HOW TO
MAKE IT BIG
IN
AUSTRALIA

D0587643

HOW TO MAKE IT BIG IN AUSTRALIA

THE DOWN-TO-EARTH GUIDE FOR HIGH FLIERS, LATE DEVELOPERS AND THE MODERATELY GREEDY

Robert Treborlang

Illustrations by Mark Knight

Major Mitchell Press

To Moi Moi's insight, wisdom and ravishing eyes

First published September 1989 by
Major Mitchell Press Pty. Limited
P.O. Box 997, Potts Point
2011 Australia

Copyright © Robert Treborlang

Edited by Derek Hornsey
Cover design by Mark Knight
Consultant: Matthew Sandblom

Typeset in 11/12 New Baskerville by
Keyset Phototype, Sydney
Typographic Consultant: Peter Hughes

Printed by The Book Printer, Melbourne

Distributed by Network to newsagencies

National Library of Australia
Cataloguing-in-Publication Data:

Treborlang, Robert
How to make it big in Australia
ISBN 0 958 7708 5 9

1. National characteristics, Australian 2. Australia — Social life and
customs. I. Title.

Contents

Intromission

ONE balmy spring night I ventured into an Australian street. The moon shone brightly over the suburb and its sea of glistening corrugated roofs. Faces peered out from behind curtains and venetian blinds. An imperceptible wind slid over the parked cars and hovered around the identical front porches.

After several failed attempts I managed to locate the street and house number I had been given for the drinks party. I entered the place with curiosity. The women clutched their bags under arm, held on to their wine glasses and tried to juggle themselves a savoury biscuit at the same time. The men stood drink in one hand, jangling keys in their pocket with the other.

Various people I had never seen before milled around me. They eyed me briefly, then went on drinking. I stood to one side, looking for a friendly face. A woman with streaked blonde hair and no handbag smiled in a cordial way. When I could find no one to introduce us, I walked up to her myself.

"Do you know any of the people here?" I said.

"Of course," she told me, "I'm the hostess."

She made an attempt to introduce me to a couple of people then disappeared into the kitchen. The first guest told me he used to be an accountant with a brewery but was now negotiating to buy a property down in the country.

"Just a house and a couple of acres."

"One can do quite a lot on two acres," I said with interest.

"Oh, it's more than two acres," he said, walking jerkily away.

The second guest was a woman who apparently had been a secretary until the previous year when she decided to branch out into some venture of her own.

"Oh, it's all getting out of hand," she said with excessive distress. "We've been expanding at such a rate that we just had to hire three more people."

"I'd love to know," I said "how exactly you mana-- "

"Ah, my God!" said the woman interrupting me and racing away towards a tall rubber tree in the corner, "isn't that a most beautiful plant!"

A little put out, I went to refill my glass. Were these people really successful? Were they embarrassed to show their success? Or did they run away because they were afraid to tell me something?

Suddenly there was a flurry at the door. A guy who appeared to be more prosperous than anyone else at the party arrived with his wife and a small entourage of eager people, obviously his employees. He walked in sun-tanned, sparkling, affluent, leading his wife whose fingers and collarbone sported lots of jewellery. Several guests put down their glasses, as if mesmerised, and approached the glamorous looking couple.

He had, I was told in whispers, survived some kind of financial crash and got everything back in just six months. Everyone thought this was very decent of him and very commendable. I for one felt intrigued. How had he done it?

Someone thought he made a fortune selling reconditioned tyres. Another told me she'd heard he had been importing frozen peas from Korea. Several people told me they were sure the man had patented a plastic substitute for corks.

"Did you see?" whispered someone behind me. "She's wearing the large diamonds which I thought she'd been forced to sell."

A short man broke out of the crowd and rushed up.

"Good to see you, mate!" he exclaimed.

At first the man who got everything back didn't seem to recognise him. No, neither the face nor the name seemed to make much of an impression. The entourage couldn't help either.

"Remember? I'm the one you still owe three months' wages to."

The man who got everything back shrugged. "I'm sorry. It must have been a long time ago."

"Long time? It's only six months!"

"Six months is a long time around here."

Very soon after this exchange, the star of the evening took his wife by the arm, gathered his entourage and left in a bustle of admiring farewells, while the man who hadn't been paid fidgeted nervously with his drink in a corner, strangely shunned by the other guests.

I asked a few people what they thought of it all.

"Sounds like a smart guy," said someone.

"Must have worked like mad to get back on top," said another.

"I work like mad too," I said, "and I am not on top."

But no one found it peculiar that although only six months earlier he had been threatened with bankruptcy and prosecution by a couple of finance companies, now he was back with a bunch of employees and an admiring audience.

What was his trick? And why was it no surprise to anyone? Did the people around me know something I didn't? And how come those he employed were so devoted to him and everyone treated him so enthusiastically?

Just what were the rules of getting ahead in Australia? Were you or weren't you supposed to be seen trying to make it? Did one show a cheery face to the world or were successful people expected to be pessimistic?

When I began to ask around, no one appeared to agree on what it meant to become successful. Some thought it was owning your own fish and chips shop. Others told me you needed to possess at least three fancy cars. While others still believed it simply meant getting paid for not having to work hard.

I was determined to find out the secret.

"No hope . . .! Give it in . . .! No chance . . .! Doomed to fail . . .! No way you can do it . . .! Save yourself the embarrassment . . .! Pathetic . . .!"

How to motivate Australians

THE surest way to motivate people in Australia to accomplish anything is to make them feel that whatever it is they are attempting to perform, it is something they couldn't possibly do.

This is your cornerstone of success in Australia. In Rumania you prod the inhabitants with exhortations such as "For the President, socialism and a kilo of sausages!" In America you just offer everyone more money. In France the best encouragement is a medal. In Iran you promise martyrdom. But in Australia you motivate people by telling them things such as:

"You haven't got a hope in hell."

"It's a lost cause."

"You'll never make it."

Should you wish to spur on a lagging sportsperson in the Soviet Union, you would exclaim: "For the Party and an apartment all of your own!" In Australia, however, you would simply utter: "Not on your life!" or "I reckon you've got less than one chance in a million," or "There's just no way you can do it."

These key words have the miraculous effect of transforming the average person from Coolangatta or Tallandoon into a high achiever. Words which might bring to a halt the overly touchy Spaniard, send into decline the hypersensitive Mongol or make the thin-skinned Indonesian lose all hope, ignite your basic Boggabrite into unrestrained action with the same

11

impetus as a powerful anabolic steroid, and they set about achieving their goals.

"What? I'll show them!"

"Just give me half a chance!"

"It makes my blood boil!"

You must understand clearly that words of traditional positive thinking have the reverse effect.

Saying "I reckon if anyone can pull it off, mate, you can," results in the person giving up after six months.

Saying "Australia's best chance for gold," results in the athlete coming fourth.

Saying "You'll knock the spots off them!" results in the pop group returning from their tour by cargo ship.

But say "You're just tilting at windmills," "Not on your Nelly!" or "You couldn't knock the skin off a rice pudding," and it becomes a different matter.

The secret is that if you put pressure and responsibility on the shoulders of Australians they panic or go to pieces. Expressions such as: "You'll kill 'em!" and "It's in the bag" and "Hot favourite" have the opposite of the desired effect by applying the constraint of having to perform. But take away the urgency and the obligation and your Australians blossom like an orange tree without a black plastic bag over it.

"I think you've shot your bolt."

"You can try until the cows come home."

"You've as much chance as a fart in a windstorm."

Suddenly they feel uplifted, responsibility is taken off their shoulders, and they experience a primeval energy release in their minds and bodies.

"Who do you think you are?"

"Just give me half a chance!"

"I'm going to teach them a lesson they'll never forget!"

Hell hath no fury like an Australian scorned.

Junking friends

IF your colleague, boss or partner irks you, don't bother to fight it out. There's no need for a slow acrimonious build up of graduated arguments, fights and remonstrations. Just a few brief weeks of mulling and then bingo! a strike, a resignation or a divorce. You must never give warning with little complaints, let alone attempt to sort it out. You must strike suddenly in order to catch the other side unawares and unprepared. Then junk them.

If friends annoy you, don't bother to sort it out. Junk them. If you can't stand the awful sandals one of them wears, or the hairstyle someone adopted, junk them along with the whole group. Look upon the process as a garage sale and make it clear that you're not junking friends for profit but to simplify life. Australians know it's best to travel light. Friends slow you down after a while.

After all, what would you say to a friend whom you are not inviting to a party?

"They're not your crowd."

"I reckon they would make you feel nervous."

"I'd rather meet you on more intimate terms. At a pub."

You should always junk your friends as soon as you change jobs. Your true friends want the best of everything for you and they all realise that there comes a seasonal time when you've got to junk them in order to

"*Mum, how many times have I told you that my new wage bracket has taken me beyond a chop and three vegies...?*"

move up in the world.

Announce that you're holding a spring clean. Since you've got a new job and you are moving to a different location, everything will have to go. Including old friends.

And when someone you haven't seen for a few weeks suddenly confronts you with: "What happened to the crowd I used to see you with?" look serious, communicate your profound regret on the matter with a sigh and reply: "Oh, I've outgrown them" or "I've moved on since then."

It's praiseworthy to junk your whole group of friends, your past, your family, whole suburbs because:

(a) others want to remain in their situation and you don't wish to disturb their peace of mind;

(b) you earn more than they do; and

(c) you are a maturing type serious about success.

How to build on shaky foundations

ON the West Coast of America and in Japan they had to devise ways to construct buildings that could withstand the earthquakes that plague those regions. In Venice they had to devise ways to build elaborate streets and palaces on the marshy lands of the lagoon. In Australia, similarly, you must learn to build on shaky foundations.

Australia is a young and changing society and your foundations may not always be quite as steady as you would wish. Like in all such situations you have to tread very lightly, take wary steps, develop a brand new set of approaches and come up with a few lateral solutions. Here are some suggestions.

1 Make sure to get into a business you know nothing about. This way you won't be prejudiced by old-fashioned or outmoded ideas regarding what works and what doesn't. Stodgy and dull Europeans might argue and debate for years and sometimes even decades whether or not a particular scheme is feasible before embarking on it. Australians, by contrast, have abandoned the prejudices of the old world and are quite prepared to plunge into enterprises without a second glance.

2 Don't look into deals to see whether or not they are viable. Do things for the joy of it. Australians know that if you make too many enquiries before you commit yourself you might find out some unpleasant facts and be discouraged.

   "It's a lovely house."

"Did you get a building report?"
"You can tell it's sound just by looking at it."
"Did you have a pest inspection done?"
"The people we're buying from assure us it isn't necessary."
"What about vacant possession?"
"The squatters promised to leave once we're ready to move in."

3 Be supremely confident about everything and explain that it is the only way to do things. Should you begin a new project, be excited about the outcome then pass the work on to someone else. This is called *knowing how to delegate*. Lose interest in projects just as they are about to reach completion. This is called *going on to bigger and better things*. Don't spend time consolidating plans, time is too valuable.

4 Highly ceremonious Asians will insist on meeting people under the most formal circumstances and then will only trust those recommended by people they've known since childhood. In Australia, however, you must be ready to drop all formality and feel quite happy to enter into partnership with people you ran into during your lunch break.

5 In Australia you will not get credit unless you are in debt. Make sure you never pay cash for anything. Keep tabs on all the people you owe money to and if necessary bring them in to your bank to act as witnesses. Make your motto: "Live for today — tomorrow you probably can't afford it."

"I've just formed this great partnership with a guy who says he can get us into fast foods...!"

19

The art of over-extending yourself

THE national art in Switzerland is yodelling from great heights. In Hungary, painting colourful flower motifs on everything in sight. In Brazil, inventing ever-harder-to-remember dance steps. In Kenya, carving rows of ebony elephants linked trunk to tail.

In Australia the national art is over-extending yourself.

In countries such as China or Ethiopia, where over-population or war has produced a scarcity of food, the skill to use every edible scrap has become an art form. Similarly, in Australia, where savings are scarce, everyone has developed the art of borrowing on everything from last year's unsettled insurance claim to next year's anticipated tax-refund.

No matter what their income level, people in Australia are fully over-extended. The same zeal once used to colonise the continent, build the Indian-Pacific railway and irrigate vast tracts of land, is now applied to borrowing right across Australia from Abbotsford to Perth.

Talented and inventive, Australians have developed the art of over-extension with true pioneering gusto. Devotees of the craft, found throughout the continent from Darwin to Humpty Doo, have caught their strong aesthetic creed in the pithy saying:

"Why save when I can borrow?"

After all, saving can be tedious, time-consuming and full of effort, whereas borrowing, or rather over-extending yourself, has nothing but advantages:

1 You can afford an impressive life-style with a minimum of physical exertion.

2 You are certain to acquire exciting new friends as there are so many other people around in the same situation.

3 Your credit cards work everywhere and if they don't someone else's will.

Analogous to the great culinary masters of the East who can transform something as mundane as a carrot into a beautiful rose, the great Australian exponents of the art of over-extending yourself, whose mastery at borrowing merits them the title of Living National Treasures, have discovered ways of converting the smallest asset into a fabulous life-style.

"I decided to put a ten percent deposit on my new bachelor flat and then took out a second mortgage to pay for my overseas holidays."

"Well, I showed them my fishing gear and they lent me the money to buy a trawler."

Tried and true connoisseurs of the difficulties involved, Australians look up to those who have successfully over-extended themselves as much as the French esteem their philosophers and Russians worship their war-heroes. "One minute he was just this guy with a nine-to-five job and the next thing you know he had managed to borrow more than most people earn in a lifetime."

How to be loyal

A NATION is made great by the loyalty of its citizens to a noble and mutual cause.

In Japan you are loyal to the Company. You start each dawn with the eight verses of the Company song, toil hard alongside your colleagues for ten to twelve hours, then drink a litre of sake with the same colleagues after hours till midnight. For your five-day annual holidays you all go away together to a work-motivation camp where you discuss, naturally, the production problems of a company you know you will stay with for the rest of your life.

In Italy, on the other hand, you're loyal to the Family. Yours, that is. One uncle owns the angora goats that another uncle shears and brings to the village where aunts and cousins weave the wool into cashmere, which when brought to town father cuts into patterns which your six brothers and sisters sew into exclusive outfits to be sold around places like Australia under a David Jones label.

In the Soviet Union, of course, you are loyal to the Party. It is the Party that provides you with special foods such as bread, butter and sausages in exclusive stores with coverings on the floor; that provides your kids with unique schools heated in winter; that provides your spouse with health resorts set in attractive villas that once belonged to class enemies.

In Australia loyalty is seen in a totally different light.

Here allegiance to any *party* is pointless because none of them will provide you with much in the way of luxuries, schools or lodgings, things which, in any case, are more easily obtained in Australia by borrowing money from a bank or credit union. Devotion to the *family* is also superfluous as by staying at home you will only get in the way. Besides, Mum and Dad are already under enough stress from each other. And it's certainly not necessary to show loyalty to the *company* you work for since by moving on to a new position you are not only vacating the job for someone else but reducing unemployment as well.

In Australia your loyalty is to brand-names.

Here words such as Vegemite, Aeroplane Jelly and Violet Crumble inspire the same fervour and arouse the same high adrenalin level that terms like *partiya, famiglia* or *chosei* do to the body chemistry of overseas loyalists.

Just as Poles in exile become all tearful at the sight of the beloved red and white flag of their nation, Australians away from their home country go jelly-like in the knees at the mere sight of a Vegemite red and orange label.

Very early in life children in a place such as Northern Ireland learn to be loyal to the Protestant or Catholic parties of their respective backgrounds. In Nicaragua kids become aware at a tender age that they have to choose between loyalty to the Sandinistas or the Contras. Similarly in Australia, even in isolated outback places, your childhood loyalties are established at a tender age between Kelloggs and Sanitarium, Fountain and Rosella, Cadburys and Nestles, Peters and Streets.

Since Australians are no less fiercely loyal than overseas zealots, if you love Vegemite you simply don't eat Marmite; Monte Carlo aficionados won't have a bar of Iced Vo Vo's; while Fosters drinkers avoid Tooheys like the plague. It's all out war between Brut and Old Spice splashers. Tampax wielders won't go near a Modess. Ansell fans won't touch a Durex with a ten foot pole. Generations of Holden enthusiasts wouldn't be seen dead in a Ford.

Your favourite brand names stay with you for life and allegiance to them proves your steadfastness of character to everyone. Successful persons in Australia always know to trot out their loyalties at the right moment in

order to create the correct impression:

"Oh, I've eaten Aeroplane Jelly from the time I was six, and haven't tried anything else ever since."

"No matter how poor we were I would only use Kleenex toilet rolls in the bathroom."

"I don't go for any of these fancy cheeses, just give me a slice of Coon."

You are also expected to maintain your brand-name loyalties right through your rise to the top to show that underneath you are really an acceptable, ordinary Australian. Hence though you may drink a French cognac like Courvoisier in private, in public you still go for Vic Bitter or XXXX. And though you may wear an original Swiss-made Rolex, point out that it is held on by your favourite Woolworths watchband.

The perfect job

ASK a contented Norwegian about his particular occupation and he would most likely tell you the precise size of the trawler he works on, the type of seasonal fish he and his six colleagues catch, the amount they haul in, the kind of nets they employ and the specific tasks he is expected to perform.

Ask a dedicated Swiss about her job and she will answer you with the particulars of the bank that employs her, what her position is, where she stands in the company hierarchy, what her exact duties are, how long she's been employed and how many years before she expects to receive a promotion.

Satisfaction and personal success in Australia are measured in completely different terms. After all, while the rest of the world was still groaning under the yoke of post-war reconstruction, Australians were already enjoying the world's shortest working hours.

For this reason in Australia it's not the actual job a person holds but the time off from it that indicates a person's status. You can recognize successful Australians by the way in which they discuss their careers.

"I've got a great job."

"Oh yeah?"

"I don't have to start work till ten in the morning."

"Well, I'm usually off by five to four."

"But we get every third Friday off."

"We get three days off before we need a medical certificate."

"We get automatic compo for five days."

"I get two bonus flexie days a year."

"I get seasonal bonuses AND tea money."

"Our strikes are fully subsidised."

"My redundancy payments include six months of unused canteen allowance."

"My termination payout gives me one work-free year."

Other topics that may be brought up successfully in conversation are long service leave, study leave, birthing class leave, maternity leave, paternity leave, holiday leave loading, superannuation, housing subsidies, low interest company loans and the free use of a car on weekends.

With a little adroitness you can avoid all mention of what either of you actually does for a living.

Transaction rituals

AUSTRALIANS take pride in their open style of business dealings and consider themselves world leaders in the field of honest transactions. Job interviews, commercial dialogues as well as business discussions in Australia are straightforward events that unfold in a most informal manner.

It would be a mistake, however, to take this congenial and open manner for granted. Australians may appear to be unaffected and casual but wherever they meet, be it in offices, pubs, clubs or television interviews, they perform several distinct ceremonial manoeuvres in the manner of mating bower birds.

The One-of-the-Boys style transaction consists of treating all prospective clients, bosses, employees or partners as if they have just arrived from Oodnadatta. The essential step here is to pay no heed whatsoever to the other person's likes, interests, biases or fears. People from overseas face some serious spiritual and bodily bruising unless they quickly learn to adjust to the terms of intimacy, first-name address, rib-punching, backhand slapping and merry ridicules that accompany such transactions.

"No flies on you, Wolfgang, you bastard!"

"Aw, give it a go, Sadahiko, get that down your gizzard."

"Not a bad possie, eh mate, Mahmoud?"

It's useful to understand that the general aim here is

to impress upon everybody that all people are basically much the same but especially so in Australia. The exchange often takes place at a race track or nightclub on company expense and the interchange continues until one of the parties feels violently ill or collapses completely.

The Full On style is practised by Australians who behave in an overly aggressive manner in order to disguise uncertainty about what exactly people want or are after. Exchanges that you might adopt in the course of such encounters are:

"I'm awake-up to you, matey."

"Come on, stop bunging on an act."

"I didn't come down in the last shower."

"You couldn't knock the skin off a rice pudding."

"What do you think you're trying to pull?"

"You couldn't give away blood at a lice picnic."

"Well, I reckon you're up shit creek without a paddle."

"You're lower than a worm's belly."

"You're as shady as a rat with a parasol."

The Full On style serves to slowly pump confidence into all parties concerned while giving them time to think.

The Devil's Advocate style consists of permanently taking up a contrary position to the other person. One party always opposes whatever the other one is saying, in the name of Truth. Practised particularly by members of the media, the Devil's Advocate style proves that neither bias nor favouritism tinges your judgment.

"I've just discovered a cure for cancer."

"Have you thought of the consequences?"

"I beg your pardon?"

"The doctors, nurses and other staff you'll put out of work?"

"Well, actually..."

"The technicians and hospitals out of action?"

"Steady on..."

"The morticians and lawyers who will go broke?"

"But the world's been seeking the cure for centuries!"

"I suppose you did it on a grant, eh?"

The Excessively Friendly style is practised by Australians from all walks of life interviewing aspiring candidates for positions vacant, for tenders or grants, for bank loans or for partnership offers. The procedure involves a lot of sympathetic body language, quiet conspiratorial asides and little verbal nudges.

"Yeah, your prospects look pretty good."

"I think you're really suited for the job."

"I'll certainly be pushing your cause."

Should you encounter such behaviour, beware immediately that you have made an unfavourable impression. Interviewers most likely think you pushy. The moment the atmosphere becomes matey, relaxed and informal, you can be fairly sure that your prospects are slim indeed. The job is definitely going to someone else. You certainly haven't got that contract. In fact you're not even in the race.

The Aloof style is a stiff manner employed when holding interviews, board meetings, staff meetings and grant applications. Movements are jerky, eyes are averted and the voice is hollow.

"I don't think you understand the situation."

"I'm afraid I don't agree with you."

"You're wrong there."

In Europe such contentious remarks are a fairly good indication of the futility of a situation. Aloof behaviour on the part of your basically easygoing Australians simply means that you have made an excellent impression, that you may be fairly sure of landing that uncertain contract, or that a promotion is most likely coming your way.

Do not fall into the trap of trying to be amicable. Make sure you don't try to warm up the situation with any friendliness. To the trick question "Any questions?" make sure you do not answer anything, shrug your shoulders and stare out the window.

In this situation ensure that there is no eye contact whatever. In Australia the only people who look their employers in the eyes are desperate ones.

The Difficult Beginnings style of exchange is very common in Australia and takes place between two people who wish to do business together, but at first are scared of each other. Then as the meeting wears on you warm up to one another.

"Hey, you're not a bad bloke/sort/person."

"You're not so bad yourself."

"I think we could do business together."

"I'm sure we could."

"We'll get on great guns."

"Like a house on fire."

"Like fleas on a bandicoot."

"We'll show 'em."

"My oath."

The exchange continues until you are so comfortable in each other's company that you can skip the business part altogether and go out instead and have a beer.

How to make excuses

WHEN apologetic Mediterranean acquaintances in Valencia, Salonika or Alexandria exclaim in their sincerest and loudest tones: "I know I swore and promised to be here at ten o'clock, however the reason I am three hours late is due to a most unhappy chain of events," you can be fairly certain that:

(a) the grandmother in question died ten years earlier;

(b) the douche-bag wasn't in the next apartment; and,

(c) the parrot never had a chance.

In Australia excuses are made in a very different spirit. Here such mundane and petty excuses would never pass muster. Excuses in Australia should either be on a grand scale or simply not made at all. Australians generally are mistrustful of those who do not get caught up in massive dramas and total disasters. This is a dramatic continent prone to spectacular catastrophes and your excuses, likewise, should reflect the violent and unpredictable nature of the environment.

"What happened?"

"I've been trying to get hold of someone at the dress shop but the woman was caught in a flash flood over the weekend and hasn't come back yet. I phoned the sales manager with the courier company but his father-in-law had just been struck by lightning. And the girl from the hotel I gave the money to has flown off to Cachexia in Brazil to look for her missing children."

"What about the theatre tickets?"

"Good God, we've made it to your party!... I know we're a bit late but drought hit us soon after departure, killing most of the livestock and we would have been here sooner if the diseases brought on by the following floods hadn't hit us at the corner of your street, not to mention the plague of insects and the..."

"Oh, my God! I must've lost them in the ambulance...!"

In many countries you are not expected to keep promises. In Australia, a country strong on Protestant ethics and Catholic conscience, you are. So how does one get out of them? How do you explain why the delivery cannot be made on time and in the quantities expected? "I've got a teeny problem with this item. There has been a bit of a production hiccup — the workers walked out on me and set fire to the factory, looters took most of the stuff and the police pinched the rest" — this might be a dandy excuse in Latin America but in Australia it makes a little too much sense. Go for the lateral approach.

"I couldn't possibly have fulfilled the order and I'm on the point of a nervous breakdown. My partner is threatening to go on holidays and I was incapacitated for three weeks. My secretary ran off with another boke and took the typewriter as well. I came back and there was all this dough missing from petty cash. The Cafe Bar broke down and now the rental company is threatening to repossess the answering machine."

Now observe a very simple rule emerges from all this. In Australia the more monstrous and unbelievable the excuse, the more likely it is to be taken as fact.

FOR THINGS THAT HAVEN'T BEEN DONE

"It's all ready, waiting for you."
"Great!"
"But I don't know where my assistant put it."
"I'll call back in an hour."
"Actually she's not coming back today."
"See you tomorrow then."
"The truth is I gave her the sack."
"So, how are you going to find it?"
"I might give the police a ring."
"The police?"
"She could have been carrying it when they fished out her body."

FOR THINGS THAT YOU HAVE NO INTENTION OF DOING

"I'm afraid I haven't had a chance yet."
"But you said Monday."
"Sorry, I've had a dreadful morning."
"Shall I ring back tomorrow?"
"As a matter of fact the other chap's gone off sick and I'm on my own here at the moment."
"At the end of the week perhaps?"
"Actually, we've had a lot of trouble with the computer."
"Next week then?"
"Well, that's when we're supposed to have the auditors in."
"How about a month from today?"
"We'll be moving premises then."
"What about December?"
"What about if *I* ring *you*?"
"When?"
"Let's make it next year just to be safe."

The aim of an excuse in Australia is to show people how much you respect them. The worthier they are, the more elaborate your story. Conversely, of course, you only tell the abrupt truth to those you hold in low esteem.

The Dynamic Entrepreneur

AN education can be a severe handicap when it comes to making money. The Dynamic Entrepreneur has graduated from the school of hard knocks and draws on facts only if all else fails.

Ensure you don't have too many skills. They would only interfere with your infallible sense of always making the right choices.

Practise greed without restraint and without embarrassment. Don't have one car, have six. Preferably all Rolls Royces. When you entertain it is always on a huge yacht. If you hold a birthday party for your wife or partner, make sure that it is reported in all the papers.

In an ordinary Australian covetousness and rapacity are considered unseemly. Their families would despise them for it, their colleagues would turn away from them. By contrast, the Dynamic Entrepreneur is allowed to practise greed. And the more greed he practises the more Dynamic he is.

Announce that money is not really important, it is merely the means to achieving a dream. And the dream is to become the richest person in Australia.

The Dynamic Entrepreneur should constantly be seen to be buying things, whether buildings, private planes, famous paintings or thoroughbred horses. Where does the money come from? No one will care. In fact the public will only care when they notice that you are *not* buying.

You have to be perpetually optimistic, especially when things aren't going too well: "Yeah, mate, future prospects are brilliant, the outlook is bloody outstanding. Timely actions taken in other places have really raised revenue expectations."

Average Australians are loath to tell you how much they earn, how much they paid for a car, how much they spend on beer. It's the opposite with the Dynamic Entrepreneur. Following much soul searching he has overcome the average Australian's reticence to talk about money matters and gives everyone the figures only too willingly. You've got a two thousand dollar suit, your one hundred foot yacht cost five million dollars, servicing your cars costs the equivalent of fifty people's annual wages.

A modicum of down-to-earthness is highly recommended, because you have to demonstrate that the tedious vulgarities of income and social position have not spoilt you a whit. Uttering a few words such as *mate*, *dinkum*, *struth* as you are speeding away to an important meeting is considered unbelievably charming.

It is also a good idea to own a modest little holding family trust which occasionally sells the public company of which you are the Chairman highly prized just slightly under-water real estate in the North of Queensland and vast tracts of barren land in Western Australia reported to contain significant untapped quantities of gorillium.

The Dynamic Entrepreneur is known for his outspoken, exacting attitude not only towards the truth but also towards those who might try to suppress it. Not for you the weak and ineffectual language used by everyone else.

"We bailed out of that project at least two and a half years ago to pursue other interests, as they say, but we are still trying to paper over the cracks and pull their hot chestnuts out of the fire."

The Dynamic Entrepreneur does not have any fixed long term plans because that would be "counter-productive." Go with the current. Roll with the punches. But whatever profits you do achieve, make it abundantly clear to everyone concerned that it was your intention to reach those targets all along.

Above everything, the Dynamic Entrepreneur is always right.

Why you shouldn't work in the field you're trained in

PEOPLE in other countries work hard so that they can get somewhere. In Australia people work hard so they can get away from it and do something else.

Australia is a modern and progressive nation where new work ethics apply. You have far greater career prospects if you hate what you do. It means that you are broadminded and open to any offers that may come along. People who claim that they actually enjoy their work and are having fun soon get their comeuppance. They are looked on as narrow-minded and amateurish and not taken seriously at all. This is because as children Australians have been taught that if something is enjoyable then probably it's not only bad for them but weakens their character as well.

As a result Australia is full of architects who hate buildings, farmers who hate the land, publishers who hate books and waiters who hate people.

Proud, freedom-loving beings, Australian workers hate to be thought of as slaves to their profession. To earn the respect of your colleagues, therefore, it's important to always have another out. Make it clear to everyone that though you have a great job you are secretly planning to:

(a) mine for opals at Coober Pedy
(b) run a fishing trawler off Cairns
(c) open a hairdressing shop in Wagga.

Best to look for a job you have no expertise in whatsoever. Remember that Australia is a pioneering nation and here people think it a sign of intelligence to have succeeded in a profession they never trained for.

When choosing an apprenticeship or course of study, pick a field you have no intention at all of being involved in.

BRICKLAYER

MD. PhD. BSc.
BEc. LLB. MA.
DipEd. BA.(Hon)
Telephone: 789890

Australians study, of course, as assiduously as the rest of the world. Everyone is very keen to acquire the profession which they know they are not going to practise. Parents are especially eager for children to do this.

"You should always have a trade, Bianca, to fall back on."

"You never know, Tom, when being a dentist might come in handy."

"It's a good idea to have a few apprenticeships up your sleeve, Trent."

Should you happen to train as an opera conductor there is every chance that your real success will come from the manufacture of plastic sewerage pipes. As a well-trained psychiatrist or pediatrician you owe it to your self-respect to make a fortune on the property market. Should your background be nuclear physics you might try your luck patenting an impermanent tattoo for teenagers. After four years of training as a sailmaker, could you hope for any more self-satisfying job than renovating pubs in Tibooburra?

Or you may choose to change professions several times in a lifetime.

"I've come to complain about the cupboards you installed."

"Sorry, can't help you."

"Aren't you the carpenter?"

"That was last week. I'm into tree surgery now."

"What am I going to do then?"

"Tell you what. I've got a mate I trained with at cookery school who's thinking of giving up his hair-dressing practice and getting into home decorating. Why don't you give him a call?"

All in all, your ambition should be to become the complete suburban renaissance person — multi-faceted, multi-talented and multi-jobbed.

The Australian Rhythm Method, or How to put things off

THE distinctive principle that governs decision-making on the Fifth Continent must be studied by all those who wish to reach any real success here, and understood by those who wish to have insight into the secret life of the nation.

When the Vietnamese need to make a decision to do something, they panic a little, deliberate a little and then carry out the task promptly and without regrets. The French will make a decision almost instantaneously because they don't want anything to interfere with their love-life or gastronomical pleasures. Americans make decisions promptly because they live in mortal fear of missing out on profits.

Practised Australians, on the other hand, know that the best method to cope with decision-making is to put things off for as long as possible. After all, this way you are not going to make any mistakes.

"Must have you over at our place sometime."

"I can do the essay the night before it's due."

Uniquely Australian, the urge to delay, defer and not decide to act just yet is as much part of the nation's heartbeat as a six-stroke Holden engine.

"Let's all have a good think about it first."

"Should get together one day and talk things out."

"Can I phone you back?"

All great nations pulsate to an inner cadence which regulates the rhythm of their lives and destinies. To randy Brazilians this pulse is defined by the orgiastic beat of the *samba*; to melancholy Portuguese by the despondent measure of the *fado*; to quixotic Poles dreaming of independence for four hundred years by the frenzied pace of the *mazurka*.

Australia's secret inner rhythm is defined by the beer commercial. The principle behind the beer commercial decrees that no matter how great their level of activity, speed, bustle, animation, briskness, vigour, push, drive, pep or energy, what Australians really aspire to is inertia.

You must learn, therefore, to pace yourself. Putting things off must become as second nature to you as sleeping is to wombats. The idea is to deliberately rhythmically delay, postpone and put off taking action until the whole decision making effort grinds to a halt.

Like a classical tragedy this process has five distinct acts or stages:

1. It's important to slow things down right from the start. When the garbage piles up, suggest squashing beer cans really flat so you only have to throw the garbage out once a week. When rain pours in through the roof, resort to blocking holes with shopping bags. "Plastic is probably even more resilient than tiles." Accompany all proposals with little self-congratulatory remarks to convince everyone that everything's under control:

"Hey, why didn't I think of it before?"

"The answer was there before our eyes!"

"We're really lucky that I've come up with this idea."

"Yes, well, that may be so, but if I don't sleep in an extra half hour how am I going to be refreshed enough to think of a solution?!..."

2. Slow things down further by looking for lateral solutions. In other words solutions that require more talking than doing. "There's no point in halting sewerage flowing onto the beach unless we can work out how to stop the process once and for all."

Convince yourself and others that the task isn't urgent. Nip it in the bud.

"Surely we have more important things to do than fret about a few cancelled orders?"

"All places this size have damp troubles in winter."

"I don't think a meeting is going to mend these broken pipes."

"It's only temporary soil erosion."

If people panic about a crack in the bloc wall make it clear that there's no urgency whatsoever. "They've been predicting the fall of the tower of Pisa for eight hundred years."

3. Put off the decision to take action for an indeterminate time, because of insurmountable difficulties. "I don't care how urgent it is, I just don't think we should oppose tree-felling around here unless we're going to come up with a substitute for paper."

Warn everyone of the immensity of the obstacles involved. "There's no point in covering the hole in the roof with new tiles unless they're going to match the old ones and they haven't made these type of tiles since Menzies was Prime Minister."

Demonstrate the wastefulness of trying to cope with something you have no control over. "What's the point of making a firebreak around the house when just one flying spark is enough to set it alight?"

If people are still not swayed, take the total disaster approach. "All right, we do make the corruption public, but what's to guarantee that the whole police force is not going to crumble like a pack of Weet-Bix?"

46

4. Place the blame for not taking a decision squarely on the shoulders of others. "Sure we should do something about these pot holes but how can we given existing council regulations?"

Spread the responsibility around. "The whole place from the front room to the dunny is in danger of collapse but nobody seems to care!"

Make it general. "If it was just our products that were returned I would say let's do something about it, but it's the whole footwear industry."

Explain that the infestation is a widespread condition and whether the individual does or doesn't do anything about it is not going to make one iota of difference. "In the Middle Ages there was nothing at all anyone could do until the brown rats arrived and wiped out the black ones."

5. Total abandon. "I can't be bothered with my kids anymore."

Grind the need for decisions to a complete halt. "Trying to make a decision about the shipping yards was a waste of time from the first."

Make everyone accept that there is nothing to be done. "Let's face it, we couldn't have helped, welfare agencies just reach their natural end just like people."

Emphasise that even if something could have been done, it's simply too late. "It looks like the Department of Main Roads will be reclaiming the whole housing estate after all."

Everyone is happy and relieved now.

"We agreed it was in everybody's interest to do nothing."

"The truth is we simply weren't ready to make a decision."

"I don't know what came over us to even consider it."

The best hours of business

COMPARED to other nations Australia is a free and informal country where business is transacted virtually at any time and under any conditions. I realised this when making my first tentative enquiries regarding the best hours for getting in touch with people.

"Take my advice," said a friend. "You can contact people in Australia any time you wish but just don't ring today."

"Why not?"

"It's Monday morning."

I was intrigued. "What happens Monday mornings?"

"Everyone is too busy telling each other about their weekend."

Grateful for the tip, I promised to heed my friend's suggestion. Since then I have found, however, that for maximum efficiency the following times, apart from Monday mornings, are also not particularly good for business:

Monday afternoons: Because the pleasure of talking about the weekend has worn off and people are suffering from the shock of returning to work after a break. Everyone is grumpy.

Tuesday mornings: Because it's when you do Monday's work.

Tuesday afternoons: The first chance everyone's had to catch up with the boss.

Wednesday mornings:	You're on top of the crest looking down at the next distant weekend. Everyone has to go to the pub or out shopping to buck up their spirits.
Wednesday afternoons:	Catching up with work you should have done on Wednesday morning.
Thursday mornings:	Takes all morning to get your pay.
Thursday afternoons:	Since it's payday everyone will stay a little longer at the pub. Afterwards they'll be in a good mood, true, but too good to transact any business.
Friday mornings:	Everyone is too busy planning the weekend.
Friday afternoons:	Usually people take all-afternoon lunches or else return to work soused.

My mention of Saturday mornings and Sunday as possible dates for transacting business met with a terrible derisory laughter from almost everyone.

"You've got to be joking! It's the weekend!"

How not to say get lost

THE Chinese are always careful to point out that theirs is the subtlest language in the world, wherein each word may be spoken in four different tones that correspond to four different and distinct meanings. Australians, with a country the size of continental China, are no less sophisticated in their use of language.

As a case in point take the word "mate".

The Standard Oxford Dictionary attributes no less than seven different meanings to the word "mate", all clearly distinct from each other. Undeterred by this Australians have proceeded to generate a further series of interpretations. The result has given birth to a great deal of misunderstanding.

Many overseas people erroneously believe "mate" to be merely an expression of friendliness and, wishing to please Australians, employ it on all possible occasions as a signifier of their good intentions — much to the amusement of locals who, having been brought up with all the shrewd uses of the word, understand intimately its Byzantine gradations.

Here is a brief sample of the variety of local connotations:

All right, mate	Forget it
Coming, mate?	I'd rather go on my own
Good to see you, mate	What the hell are you doing here?
Good day, mate	Make it quick
How are you, mate?	You're nobody important
I'm telling you, mate	I'm lying through my back teeth

Geez, mate	How stupid can you get?
Listen, mate	You won't understand anyway
What you reckon, mate?	You better agree with me on this or else
Hang on, mate!	Shut up or I'll bash your face in!

So if you wish to get rid of someone as they appear in the doorway of your workshop, office, home, room, it's easy to make them uncomfortable:

(a) open the door wide

(b) look them straight in the eye

(c) using a broad sweeping gesture usher them in with a cheery "Come in, mate!"

Any sensitive well-behaved Australian will know immediately that what you really mean to say is "I wish you would get lost."

The national industry

EVERY country worthy of being called a nation possesses one particular industry that provides people with the main source not only of their revenue but also of their civic pride. In Nauru the national industry is mining bird droppings rich in superphosphate. In Taiwan, assembling half-priced American-style computers. In Rumania, pickling and bottling gherkins.

In Australia the national industry is cheating the government.

This high-growth enterprise with a rate of expansion that is the envy of the Western World provides both direct and indirect employment to a huge section of the population. Company directors and receptionists, accountants and bankrupts, plumbers and doctors, artists and dock workers, lawyers and criminals, butchers and politicians, financial advisors and little old ladies, all toil to make the Australian national industry what it is today.

The national industry will look after you from the time you leave school till well after retiring age. No matter how small the scale you begin with, you can soon find a profitable niche depending on your interests and ingenuity.

"How did you go this year?"

"I managed to claim for my daughter's pet wombat."

"Yeah, well, next time you should go the whole hog."

Do not get fooled by the old adage: "Nothing is certain in the world except for death and taxes." Though the first claim might yet be investigated (sometimes a miraculous revivification has taken place of individuals long thought dead who reappeared magically to head small mining consortiums in Western Australia), the second one has definitely been proved wrong due to the concerted dedication of Australians, so that the adage now reads: "Only two things are certain in Australia, death and tax fiddles."

The sharpest and most daring have made a dramatic discovery. Known as the Australian Taxation Corollary it dictates that the larger your company, the less the amount of payable tax. Conversely, the smaller the company, the greater the amount of deductions. The corollary also states that tax can be paid in two basic ways:

(a) As little as possible.

(b) None at all.

Remember that no matter how paltry the fiddle you begin with, this is a country of limitless opportunities and your own success in the national industry depends merely on the confines of your boldness. While in other parts of the world experts may believe that the last word in tax rorts has been spoken, Australians from all walks of life dedicate more energy to cheating the government than to any other national endeavour.

A considerable part of your time ought to be spent not only hiding your true earnings from the government but also inventing persons earning them. It's important that you should do business or be employed under various names in order to increase the size of Australia's working population. Humble but hardworking Australians apply themselves very seriously to this task.

"If someone rings for Phil say I'm at the brewery."

"All right."

"If they ask for Ron tell them I've gone to get the bricks."

"Very well."

"If a woman wants Bill find out the age of the car."

"Fine."

"And if they inquire after Bob say I've bought the pipes."

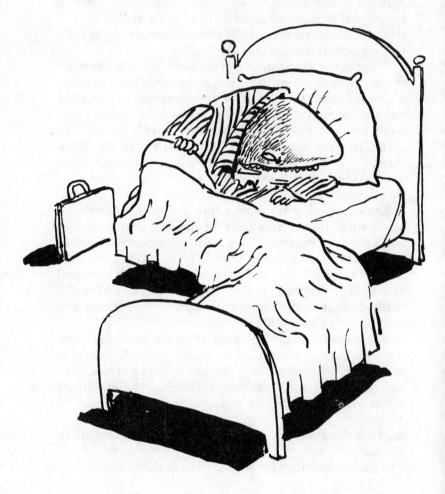

Couldn't lie straight in bed.

"Great."

"And if you want me at the factory better ask for Mac."

"OK."

"Now are you sure you can remember all that?"

"No worries, Grandpa."

This technique may be applied especially to the field of social security benefits, compensation and welfare. Apply for assistance under three or four names in order to keep the industry buoyant. With a little effort it is possible to simultaneously work under one name while claiming under several others a permanent disability pension for an incapacitated spine, and live in public housing while you are paying off your home.

Not only are the nine governments of Australia willing to encourage the national industry, successful industry members also never miss an opportunity to claim assistance with some cashgrant from one government or another. The country is full of individuals with a long established knowledge in the field and it would be wise to trust yourself to one of these experts to guide you through the many available avenues.

"I understand you can help me obtain a government cash-grant."

"Have you a farm?"

"I don't think so."

"Don't worry, I've six people ready to swear that you've got one."

"Why?"

"Because the government likes people to have bilberry farms and is willing to pay for the privilege of seeing people establishing them."

"I see."

"And very few have claimed for farms this year."

"Oh."

"And the money set aside for them could easily get lost."

"So?"

"So to save the government the wastage..."

Modern-day pioneers from all over the globe, lured

by the glitter of Australia's national industry, are also keen to be part of the action. Like the bounty-hunters of old who roamed the Wild West, a great number of New Zealanders, British, Americans, Germans, Chinese and Japanese criss-cross the seven states of Australia in audacious search of generous government endowments.

"What do you mean a floating dock subsidy?"

"I only need help of a hundred thousand."

"But you're an hour's drive from Alice Springs!"

"All right, fifty thousand."

"And your registered company address is a hut in the desert!"

"Very well, I'll settle for twenty-five."

"And the only water for miles is subterranean!"

"OK, for ten thousand I'll build it underground."

How to be the minority

AUSTRALIA is, without doubt, the most egalitarian country in the Western World. Social distinctions are virtually nonexistent. Ninety-eight per cent of the population considers itself no better or worse than anyone else and is perfectly happy to live assimilated into the homogenous equality-minded community.

Unfortunately, there remains a misguided minority that seems unable to fit into the general populace. Due to a variety of historical reasons its members are unwilling to fit in and choose to live in small ghettos around the country.

If you want to make it really big in Australia you must pass yourself off as a member of this minority. It's both advantageous and profitable to be accepted as one of them because of the amount of preferential treatment and government assistance given to you if you do. Here are some notes on their background:

- It's estimated that they make up two per cent of the population. Many believe that Australia actually belongs to them. Others are convinced that the country is where it is today only because of the personal sacrifices made by members of this minority.

- Most are nomadic and have to commute between multiple dwellings. When the urge comes over them they throw everything down and follow a compulsion to travel long distances, often just for a few days.

- In the old days most were made to feel ashamed of their ways, with many forced to pass themselves off as average Australians. Of course, in trying to integrate into the rest of society they often lost their identity and, sadly, much of their self-respect.

Following much international criticism, however, society at large now bends over backwards to grant as much help to this minority group as possible. The government has come to realise that just because this small percentage of the population happens to own more than sixty per cent of the nation's wealth, it doesn't mean that they should be discriminated against.

Several important steps have been taken therefore by the various governments of Australia to improve the situation of this hitherto neglected group:

1 Considerable sums of public funds, increased Commonwealth aid and assistance programmes are being deployed to improve their life-style even further. Bigger homes, larger tennis courts, helipads and several other essential features such as servants (called "staff" to please Australian democratic sensibilities) are being accorded to them in an effort to keep them happy.

2 Fortunately the government has had the intelligence to legally protect the minority's interests by passing special legislation to change old-fashioned laws that say you can't own everything.

3 Moves towards giving them extensive privileges including rights to all natural resources, crown lands, media, railroads, airlines, forests, lakes, mountains and ocean foreshores are currently under way.

Resignation

ANYONE can get a job. The real art lies in knowing how to resign.

The Japanese feel a deep obligation to stay with a company for life. In the unlikely event that someone does decide to leave, they will be looked upon as freaks and spoken of with suspicion for the rest of their days.

"Remember Yukiyama?"

"The one who resigned from Sony in '68?"

"'67 to be exact."

"What about him?"

"His son just changed jobs."

"It only goes to show."

"Tarred with the same brush."

"The apple doesn't fall far from its tree."

While not exactly bound for life, Germans sign work-contracts for periods of up to ten years. Those who break their agreements and wish to leave earlier than stipulated must face the consequences.

"Come in, Schmackelpuss."

"Yes, sir."

"I understand you wish to leave five weeks early."

"Yes, sir."

"Here are the necessary resignation forms."

"Where? In this crate?"

"Have them filled in by March."

Australian attitudes to employment are rather different. In Australia, the mobile society par excellence, after three months you are well-respected and established, while a year-long stint in a job makes you practically an old-timer. Anything over three years is looked at with suspicion.

"You've been here a while, haven't you?"

"So have you."

"I'm only staying because they give me a car."

"Oh, well, that's all right then. Me, I'm just saving up to go overseas."

In countries such as Sweden, Holland and the United States, you can improve your position by doing the right things and staying with the company. In Australia you achieve the same result by leaving it.

Conditions under which you should resign are:

(a) You don't like someone.

(b) Someone doesn't like you.

(c) They refuse your third pay rise for the season.

(d) You've stolen enough clients to start a business of your own.

(e) They announce a general audit.

(f) You're about to be fired.

At no time should you show allegiance to either employers, or fellow employees. It's not necessary because you know that by moving on you are vacating the job for someone else. In fact you are creating employment and exercising your freedom at the same time. And since Australia is a mobile society, it is the duty of every conscientious employee to keep on the move.

The French, if they wish for a career, do a step-by-step advance from dumb menial jobs until they become well-rounded professionals with a high degree of expertise. In Australia the only expertise you need is one in changing jobs.

The lead-up to a resignation is always the most crucial period of your employment. It should begin from the moment you take up your new job.

"Things look very suss to me."

"Seems they're really rapt about going broke here."

"I'd be shocked if I can stick it out."

Escalate your grumbling and complaints but be wary to do it only to people who don't matter or who can't help the situation. Clothe your distress in cryptic remarks:

"This place has more problems than a high-school maths book."

"Someone here would rat on her mother's RSI."

Remain in your job only until your first pay rise. That same week start looking for a new position which offers you more money. Should they refuse to give you another increase the way is open for you to resign immediately because they're obviously not paying you what you're worth.

"They're too mean even to hang themselves."

Take care, however, to never actually give the real reasons why you are resigning otherwise problems could get sorted out and you might be forced to stay on.

How to be the majority

IN China the majority are farm workers. In Brazil, the unemployed. In Bangladesh, flood victims. In Afghanistan, guerilla fighters. In Kuwait, rich idlers.

The majority in Australia are government employees.

Schools, universities, airlines and electricity, along with gas and water utilities, several banks, motor registries, the largest insurance companies, post offices, hospitals, libraries, trains, buses, trams, sewerage and garbage disposal services all belong to the state and are all staffed by government workers.

If you are lucky enough to be accepted into the wide ranks of Australia's local, state or federal public servants, you must be careful to uphold generations of tradition. Below are the basic attitudes you need to exhibit in order to fit happily into any of these organisations.

Remember — in the new public service there is no guaranteed tenure. This is why you must try so much harder.

1 The instant you walk in through the door of your place of employment each day, you must begin to:
    (a) look listless, care-worn and tired;
    (b) sigh;
    (c) groan.

An impression of permanent and irreversible exhaustion is the sign of true efficiency. It is the hallmark of the devoted, dutiful and hardworking Australian government employee. English public servants pretend to be efficient, Germans go for strictness, in India officiousness is probably the general rule. In Australia if you do not seem terminally tired, or

The world-famous Australian termite castles.

fatally buggered, you will simply not be taken seriously or respected by either your colleagues or the public at large.

2 Should you find yourself in a situation where your chief task is to deal with members of the general public, you must be careful to ensure that a long queue is formed at all times before anyone behind the counter resumes work. Bear in mind that Australians are a patient and well-behaved people. They never complain of having to queue up and wait since in the olden days whenever someone did speak out, every-one was punished. See how long you can hold them off. Make side bets with other employees.

3 As Australia is a vast country with a great future, you would be wise to plan carefully for long term periods. No matter which section of the public service employs you, map out your possible free days several years in advance. Outline exactly what days you will not be working on up to a decade at a time. Ensure you are always able somehow to get a day off whenever you want to. Organising flexie-time dates, preferably in massed clumps, is also a major duty. Plan sick leaves well ahead, giving special attention to synchronisation with annual and public holidays.

Great Australian inventors

AUSTRALIANS have proved to be the resourceful originators of many great scientific innovations. But while the brilliant minds that developed the Sarich Orbital Engine, In Vitro Fertilisation and Mixomatosis have received international accolades for their achievements, little or nothing has been heard of the imaginative Aussie brains who have taken on the challenge of inventing invisible diseases.

As supposedly advanced countries like the USA, Germany and Japan have virtually ignored this field, it has been left to Australia to shoulder the burden of carrying out the necessary research. Thanks to the effort of some of the nation's finest intellects, the country that gave the world the Plastic Downpipe and the Green Bean Slicer now provides everyone with equal and substantial opportunities to make it big in the field of compensation.

An arsenal of invisible diseases stands at your disposal: Kangaroo Paw, Mediterranean Back, Permanent Migraine, Gastro, Colic, Reflux, Colitis, RSI (Repetitive Strain Injury), TOAD (Tool Operating Allergy Distress) and Compensation Neurosis, to name but a few.

As a good Australian you can do your bit by inventing a new invisible disease. With luck you can build an entire career on this and even enter politics. With judicious approach you can perfect the technique of never having to work again.

Discoveries may come to the simplest of people, in the simplest of ways. You meet up with some old friends who live in luxury houses and don't seem to work very hard. Five years before they were work-mates. Now you look around and ask in amazement:

"How did you do it? I haven't even been able to save a deposit on a bachelor flat."

"That's because you go about it the wrong way."

"What do you mean?"

One of your friends takes a step nearer: "Are you sure you're feeling OK?"

"Yeah," adds another, "it's pretty hazardous work you're doing."

"No, no, I'm just packing 250 gram tins into small boxes."

"I bet there's a lot of bending and lifting."

"No, they come along an assembly line and you just pick them up and plop them in. They've even supplied us with adjustable seating."

"Adjustable, eh?" muses someone.

"Yeah, these modern contraptions can be pretty dangerous," observes another.

"I heard lots of people get their fingers broken trying to move the seats up and down," says a third helpfully.

"No, no, it's all quite easy — they're on air-cushions and there's a lever."

"A lever!" says one meaningfully.

"A lever!" echoes another. "And how many times a day do you have to bend down to move the lever?" asks the third.

Like Stevenson, Pasteur and Sarich, the inventor's inspiration strikes. "Geez, yes! What with the repetition of putting the cans into boxes and having to move the lever up and down all the time, I reckon it could be really bad for me!"

"That's right! Something like that happened to me!"

"And me!"

"And me!"

Congratulations all around.

Your friends are adamant. "Don't go into work any more until you fix the problem."

"But I need the job to pay my bills."

"No, mate, this is serious, what you need is to get on

Australian inventors await the judges' final decision.

top of the situation. You're not within a cooee of working for the next five years."

Take note, however, that the precise guidelines set out by the ACA (Australian Compo Association) for such inventions are stringent and must be rigidly adhered to:

1 In the early stages the malady must be undetectable by scientific means yet must still qualify the sufferer to take a couple of hours off work each day.

2 As time passes the condition must not cause any serious pain to the claimant yet should appear severe enough to support a sizeable claim for compensation.

3 The illness should have a built-in deterioration factor so that after a few months of futile treatment, a year's time off from work on full pay is the only solution.

4 The ultimate test of a good disease is whether or not it can be eventually pronounced incurable. This will permit you to live on compo for the rest of your working life.

The phone

MOST of us employ much the same clouting techniques to recover unused coins from a broken public phone-box whether we are in Brisbane or Bombay, and it is no more aggravating trying to get through to a continually engaged number in Adelaide than in Addis Ababa. There are, however, a few specific local procedures which callers ought to be conversant with since methods pioneered here over the course of the past century have made telephoning in Australia a unique experience.

As a rule Australians are friendly and cheerful over the telephone. Unlike many overseas interlocutors they welcome your call and are happy to exchange views and information. The general awareness of good phone manners is extremely high, in line with the lofty scale of civilisation reached by the entire nation. It is virtually inconceivable not to want to do business with most Australians after the friendly reception they offer callers.

Australians are also invariably keen to postpone discussions or negotiations to a further date.

Your expected and traditional course of action is to:

Agree readily on a time and date at which they are going to ring you back; and then — Forget all about it. As soon as you hang up you must not expect to hear from them again.

After years of trial and error Australian business personnel in both private and public sectors have discovered that the real aim of the telephone is to inform callers in a friendly fashion that the person they are seeking is somewhere else. Furthermore it has been

"Ring, ring... Beep, beep... Sorry, Richard is in a meeting at the
moment, so if you could just leave your number on his car phone
answering machine, his secretary will get back to you from her office
on the yacht..."

realised that if you make the whereabouts of the sought person a complete mystery then the chance of callers ever attempting to call again will be highly diminished.

"One moment please. That number is engaged. What? No, she's also gone to lunch. Who? Let me check. I'm sorry but he has gone to a meeting. I'll put you on to somebody else."

You are now talking to Somebody Else.

"I'm afraid this is not my department. Can you call later? Well, yes, I suppose I could ask. Look, why don't I transfer you and you can ask yourself."

The next person: "No, you've been wrongly transferred. I'll try to get you back to the switchboard. But I'm new here and it might take some time."

With adroit telephone management callers will either:
(a) give up in despair
(b) forget what they rang about in the first place.

The phone is a true weapon of business in Australia. You must ensure, therefore, that your staff cover your tracks at all times, and each other's as much as possible.

1 The most acceptable excuses for not answering the phone are:
   • She's out
   • He's at a meeting
   • She's away
   • He's on leave
   • She's no longer with the company
   • Deceased.

2 Organise secretaries to sit there filtering calls. Hideous tinkle of *Greensleeves* comes on while she says to her boss: "Want to talk to Bill Radovich?"

3 If you prefer the more personal approach advise secretaries and staff that no matter how often people may ring for you they should be always cheerily informed: "What a shame, you just missed her by a few minutes."

Politics

UNLIKE Britain, whose lengthy political history dictates perplexing bureaucratic structures, Australia's more recently created political system is easy to understand and simple to follow. There are nine houses of parliamentary assembly, eight non-federal houses of elected representatives, seven parliaments with upper and lower houses, six houses of elected senators, five influential parties, four arms of judiciary, three tiers of government, two branch levels to every party and one governor general.

This arrangement is, of course, not only simple and straightforward but also highly equitable to every Australian. Due to the small population of the country and the large number of politicians needed to fuel the system, your statistical chances of becoming elected, chosen, picked, designated, shanghaied, blackmailed, coaxed, nagged, plagued, irritated, exasperated or annoyed into seeking a position in Australian politics at some time or other in your life are greater than anywhere else in the world.

For this reason it's advisable to be mindful of the following basic fact.

Political parties in Brazil oppose each other in a seemingly brutish fashion. At election-time they go for the jugular without regard for truth or law; most parties grab what power they can and those that miss out retreat to plan either deadly juntas or lethal campaigns of vilification.

It couldn't happen in Australia.

Competition between opposing parties in India can become so intense and escalate to such a tumultuous

Overseas Politics

pitch that instead of candidates chasing the electors' votes it is the electorate that chases the candidates down the street armed with clubs and machetes.

It couldn't happen in Australia.

Party rivalries in Spain ended in civil war between the Falangists and the Republicans; in China, they culminated in an all out struggle between the Nationalists and the Communists; in Mexico, in a protracted war between the Conservative and the Revolutionary parties.

It couldn't happen in Australia.

Australians are careful to avoid civic conflict of any sort and are keen to see their various political parties coexisting in harmony with one another. They have agreed therefore that all political fighting should go on not between parties but *inside* them.

As in all democratic societies, this is done on a regular basis and with a high ratio of participation. Lying, cheating, back-stabbing, betrayal, treachery, disloyalty, subversion and perfidy are all used with great gusto.

Every party member thus gets a chance of a rounded view of politics and becomes familiar with the democratic political process. And since the parties are busy fighting within their own ranks they have no energy to carry out any major reforms, which means the country can remain stolid, stable and ever unchanging.

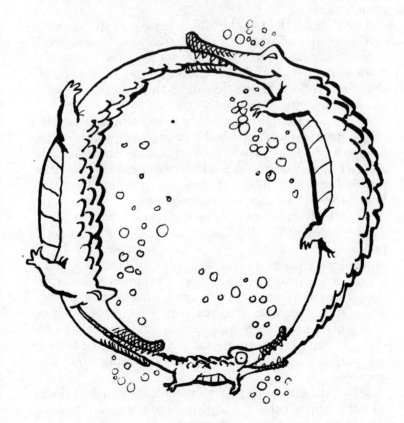

Australian Politics

The Role Model

THE Role Model is often found in the area of public relations, media and fashion. A blondish shade of hair is desirable. It's good to have been married. Twice is even better.

The Role Model has the ability to do everything. You can bring up children, be an effective wife, have several successful careers in your lifetime, act as a socially responsible person, become the supporter of important charities. Nobody knows how the Role Model copes with her busy schedule, not even she.

The Role Model's aim in life is to fulfill her needs, wants, desires, ambitions and aspirations as well as strive for spiritual self-realization. In an ordinary person such a variety of goals might lead to emotional conflict and physical exhaustion, but these things do not affect the Role Model. You can be running a high-fashion company and advertise tent-frocks at the same time.

The only conflict the Role Model ever has is not with people but with issues. With people, you may have misunderstandings or cooling off periods, you may choose to go your separate ways or progress to maturer things, but ultimately you are certain that everyone deep down still loves and admires you. With issues it is a different matter. Here you may be as aggressive and stony as you like. Stopping tall buildings or tree felling are perfectly acceptable ways of expressing your aggression.

Whatever the average person achieves is always done with the help of others. The Role Model seems to be able to achieve most things on her own.

The Role Model is also multifaceted. Manifest a sense

Half mum, half management.

of humour about everything except yourself. Declare that the purpose of a woman's life is to:

(a) Teach men a lesson, that is be on two committees more than you have time for.

(b) Be a role model to women, in other words someone who no matter how busy she is still thinks of her family's breakfast.

You have to cultivate your reputation with the greatest care. The people surrounding you are always ideal and what imperfections they might manifest such as drug-addiction, alcohol dependency, nervous disorders or depression, have proved to be blessings in disguise by turning you into a stronger person and teaching you how to cope with the difficulties that crop up in your career.

Coping with service

SAY the word "service" to Italians and they will probably visualise a waiter with six plates of food piled on each arm racing between rows of noisy customers. Service to most Chinese means a seven-course meal prepared by the time they have taken their places at a table set for twelve. To Americans, service means a twenty-five storey hotel rising out of the Kalahari Desert that offers customers ten different varieties of freshly made hamburgers at three in the morning.

Say "service" to Australians and most will think of:
- (a) John Newcombe in a Wimbledon final
- (b) a grease and oil-change for the family car
- (c) the Armed Forces, or
- (d) a long and tedious church wedding.

Australians, on the whole, are a rugged and spartan race and do not associate the concept of service with the comforts of life.

In Australia service is perceived in a very different light.

"I hate to disturb you and I know it's 12.30 and probably your lunch-break but do you think I could possibly have a look at the menu?"

For service from trades people you are well-advised to consult a reputable astrologer or numerologist to see if they will manage to turn up. Certainly booking their time, telling them it's urgent or offering more money as you would in other countries doesn't work.

Being so democratically-minded Australians do not think that one of two people with equal rights before nature and the law ought to engage of their own free will in something as humbling as service.

It's a good idea to crawl for service.

First you try to get through on the phone three or four times. Finally a voice answers. "Ah yes! I'll get someone else who knows all about spare parts."

You hang on for five minutes. A new person picks up the phone.

"Yes?"

You make your request all over again.

"Wait while I see. I'll have a look."

Ten minutes later:

"Did you say it was an '80 or an '85 model?"

"'87."

"Wait a minute."

Shuffle of feet as the person goes off to inspect the stock again. More slow shuffling as the person comes back and picks up the phone.

"There's only an '84 model. I'll have to check when they changed the design."

After another interval you find out they do have the right piece after all. It's agreed that the item will be put aside and you will pick it up as soon as possible.

You get there. It's not waiting for you.

"Excuse me."

"Hang on. I'm serving someone."

"But there's no one here."

"They've gone to the car to check on a part."

Rule One: Never let people sense that you want something in a hurry. Should Australians get the scent that you're desperate for something, in a hurry or at all keen then things will slow down to a crawl.

Fifteen to twenty minutes later it's your turn.

"There's no more parts. We're out."

"But someone told me they put one aside for me."

"Don't know anything about that."

"I was told it'll be on the counter."

"Not here."

You may insist as much as you like but no one is willing to search for anything. Finally an employee turns up whose voice is strangely familiar. Hope springs eternal.

"Waiter!"

"I am the person who phoned you earlier... Have you the part?"

"Yeah. Yeah. Just let me get organised."

Rule Two: Because Australians are a proud and independent people it's best to give an order then quickly turn aside so that they have a chance to carry out your request without feeling servile.

Some considerable time later the employee comes back and tackles the indifferent colleague.

"Where's that thing?"

"What?"

"Where did you put that part I put over here?"

"What part?"

The fight lasts anything up to ten minutes.

"What are you talking about?"

"I had it wrapped in a piece of paper."

"Oh that! It's over there. I thought it was your lunch."

Now to the price.

"I'll have to look it up."

Following a hefty wait a figure is finally established.

"There's also sales tax."

"How much?"

"Let me check."

Another wait.

"What's holding it up now?"

"We're changing over to computers."

Docket in hand at long last, you go over to the cashier.

"Geez," says the cashier, "you're lucky. We're just about to close."

Networking your divorce

IF you want to make it big in Australia then you must consider divorce. Divorce is at the basis of the Australian business experience. Like owning your first car or buying your first property, your divorce provides that all-important training ground for dealings with the legal, accounting and banking professions.

There are several stages needed to expand your network of contacts.

Stage 1. Two children and seven years down the track you take a look at your partner and realise that things aren't what they used to be. One morning over breakfast you bring up the topic of divorce.

> *Spouse:* But I thought we were happy.
> *You:* I did too.

Stage 2. After a few sessions with an impartial certified accountant and an amiable tax consultant, both sides accept that temporary separation is the best possible course of action. He agrees to give her an allowance and one of the two cars. She agrees that he has free access to their children and joint bank account.

> *One:* You take the leather Chesterfield.
> *The Other:* No, no, you take it.
> *One:* I insist.
> *The Other:* I think you need it more.
> *One:* Okay, but then I want you to have the Parker dining room suite.

The solitude of separation.

> The Other: You love music more than I do. I insist you take the Aiwa.
> One: All right, but you should keep the Blaupunkt.
> The Other: We are both going to be happy with our new decision.
> One: Life is going to be better for everyone all around.
> The Other: And we are both going to stay good friends.

Stage 3. Within two months of attending self-improvement and physical fitness classes, one has found a better and more highly paid job and the other has found somebody ten years younger, fresher and lovelier. Now it really starts.

> She: He's a bad influence on the children. (*Promptly refuses access and takes the kids to the country where he can't get at them*)
> He: She doesn't really need the car. I'd rather give it to my new girlfriend. (*Sneaks around one night and drives it away with a set of spare keys*)

Stage 4. On advice from a unbiased marriage counsellor, he spends endless amounts of time looking for receipts to prove that things were bought before they got married. On advice from an understanding psychiatrist, she gets people to search for secret bank accounts she knows he's got hidden somewhere.

> She: I'll teach him a lesson he'll never forget!
> He: I'd rather burn the sofa than let her have it!

Stage 5. Urged by a successful solicitor he tries to have himself declared bankrupt in order not to have to give her any money. She is still searching for his hidden bank accounts and, advised by a sympathetic magistrate, has the kids placed under police protection.

Stage 6. Divorce is now all the go and the respective brilliant barristers are demanding everything for their clients. The family court judge like Solomon decides to split the assets down the middle.

> *One:* (*With venom*) Very well, I'll have A to K of the Britannica set, you can have L to Z.
> *The Other:* (*With hatred*) OK, I'll have the insides of the piano and you can have the case.

Finally, it is necessary to sell the house and all the other assets anyway, in order to pay for the costs. But in the meantime the network of solicitors, barristers, removalists, analysts, guidance counsellors, think-positive teachers, physical education instructors, accountants, baby-sitters, private detectives and assorted financial advisors have become your permanent business connections, if not your life-long friends. For many, of course, divorce is often the first *and* last business experience.

On being a bully

CONFUSED and ignorant overseas visitors cannot grasp why successful business people, politicians and artists in Australia, who act as despots in private, go to so much trouble to hide this fact from the public at large. In most other countries people are proud of their bullies and hold them up as national heroes. Austrians admire nothing more than Beethoven's impossible temper. The British are prouder of their swaggering Henry VIII than of any other monarch. The domineering Morgan and Rockefeller are paragons of American business behaviour.

Don't attempt it in Australia.

Here serious musicians are admired for their savourless character, Prime Ministers for their amicability and heads of corporations for their inoffensive blandness.

If you want to make it big, therefore, your behaviour in public should be always unfailingly modest. Australia is a parliamentary democracy and you are a democratic person. Everyone's view is important. The little man or woman always gets a hearing. Do not put forward your own personal views in any discussion. Be like the Delphic oracle. Stand up for the rights of the individual, preferably of those individuals you have never met in person.

"I respect everybody."

"Won't make up my mind until I hear all sides."

"The masses have the same rights as everyone else."

You must never attack anyone in public because Australians are fair-minded people who will automatically go to the defence of the person being aggressed.

This is the reason why wise politicians, sensitive artists and affluent business people in Australia know to shout only behind closed doors and then only at favourite family members, trusted colleagues, policy advisors and party underlings, who can be relied upon for masochistic discretion. Abusing for hours on end faithful secretaries, cowed board-members, terrorised assistants and oppressed family members is all right too, as long as you do it away from the limelight in soundproofed rooms or inaccessible offices and keep the following points in mind:

1 Facial appearance is critical. Mask what is happening inside you by maintaining the same facial posture for all occasions. With muscle inflexibility, your potential range of expression can still be quite versatile:
   (a) stern
   (b) stern and red.

2 Try to sound angry and ready to explode at all times. Don't, for example, allow others to complete their sentences. Good Australians are carefully brought up by their fathers never to have the last word, so it should be plain sailing.
   "What the hell do you think you're doing?"
   "I thought I would bring the..."
   "Don't you have anything better to do?"
   "But you told me that..."
   "Listen, mate, if I need a reminder I'll ring Telecom."

3 Whenever you can, simply eliminate tenderness or gentleness from all modes of communication. Speak in statements to both family and colleagues. Make assertions in a growling manner and then walk away. You certainly don't want the other persons to mistake your staying on for weakness.

"Whaaaaat the blooooooody hell is thiiiiiis? What do you call these three green things in a box? Are you insane or something? Don't you ever do that again! Jesus that bloody carrier is late again! I told him if he is not here by ten! Oh God! Just bums! That's all can get to work with! Nothing but bums!"

4 Australians may forgive the occasional drunken sentimental outburst, but chances are they won't if you treat them with tenderness, intimacy or gentleness when sober. Just one word, phrase or sentence indicating fondness, even if said in a jocular tone with an exaggerated facial expression, may compel people to suspect that underneath you are really a softie.

You shouldn't care, of course, about the opinions of those close to you, only about the fact that someone who has met the sister of the store manager whose driver delivers your groceries should go on saying things about you such as:

"You couldn't find a nicer bloke."

"She's a true lady."

"What a terrificly democratic person."

How to be a great negotiator

NEGOTIATING in other countries means wanting to get an advantage over your opponent. The Japanese may prolong discussions for three or four years over a simple point under the guise of wishing to make a unanimous decision. Russians make sure they appear virtually abuse-proof and will come back cheerfully no matter how many times they get knocked back. The French will wine and dine you until you are so softened up that all your will to fight has drained out of your fibres. The Americans will just want to bribe you, bribe your superiors, your superiors' superiors, your family, their families, everyone's in-laws and anyone who happens to be delivering the morning papers.

Australians, by contrast, have decided to cut all the crap.

In Australia, you see, you don't need any of these advantages over your opponent since you already have one by being Australian.

Make it clear right from the start that you are a great negotiator and that you never give an inch in any transaction. It will impress all those you don't have dealings with and will give fair warning to those with whom you do.

Develop a no-nonsense uncompromising attitude. Act tough and scowl a lot. Appear completely in charge of any situation you don't understand.

"I convened this meeting to discuss the situation."
"Sure."
"We want work bans on all existing delicatessens."
"If you wish."
"No deliveries of sausages, salamis or sauerkraut."

"Boy, did I go in there and give them something during those negotiations!"

"OK by us."

"Delighted to see you're taking such a sensible attitude."

"Actually we're here to remove all the old potplants."

Not only state up front what your demands are but also make sure you do it in a forthright aggressive manner while walking in through the door.

"We want $2.15 per item."

"Well..."

"And won't take anything under $2.10."

"But..."

"Unless you make a firm offer for $2.00."

Should you happen to negotiate with Greeks there's always a good chance that sometime between the start and close of proceedings they'll get up and announce that the whole process doesn't interest them anyway, they're sorry to have gotten into it in the first place, that it was a misunderstanding all along, they don't really wish to buy, sell or settle anything. This has a pretty poor effect on your self-confidence and soon you find yourself happy to agree to whatever they say.

The Chinese concept of negotiating takes a totally different course. To begin with they'll confess that their dearest wish is to make the decision in your favour but unfortunately the verdict never depends just on them, there are others to be considered too who haven't made up their minds yet and so they'll wear you down by coming back dozens of times to ascertain price, conditions or terms. The net effect of all this, especially when stretched over a few years, is to have you crawling for mercy.

Unlike these complex practices, the rules of Australian negotiating are simple and straightforward:

1 Being democratically-minded ensure that you never distinguish between underlings and people with real influence and power. Treat them all the same.

2 Be firm but in a vacillating uncertain sort of manner. State your demands up front in strong aggressive

tones, for instance, then look quickly around the room to see if you've done the right thing.

3 Do not forget that at the sign of slightest conflict, of angry words or bluffing outbreaks from your opponent, it is only sporting to give in and sign whatever paper they place in front of you.

4 Call whatever you end up with a great victory for common sense.

An alternative school of Australian negotiating states that it's probably best not to negotiate at all, to have nothing to do with one's opponents, rivals or competitors, that it's better to ignore them completely:

"No one tells us what to do" — except for the Americans, the Japanese, the Poms, the Indonesians, the IMF, the World Heritage Council, the World Bank, the Unions and the rich.

"Success! I now possess ten times my own body weight in debt!..."

Some special tips

- When talking business don't be optimistic about the future. Only entrepreneurs and members of the government are ever optimistic and everyone knows that in Australia entrepreneur is simply a polite expression for crook.

- Don't forget that in Australia all true mates are pessimists. A mate is someone who always points out all the things that can go wrong.

- Australia is the land of equal opportunities. It is also called the land of the fair go. This means giving the job to the person most unsuited and with the least experience.

- It's all right to make long term plans, as long as you change them in a panic at the last moment based on something you overheard during lunch.

- If you imitate anything make sure to do it badly, so that no one can possibly recognise what you copied. Then you can claim originality.

- Never go for a favour to the same person twice. If you do, they'll only ask someone else to do it anyway. Remember, there are sixteen million people in Australia.

ROBERT TREBORLANG

Born in... grown up in... educated at... Robert Treborlang is admirably qualified to write on the allure of making it big in Australia. He practises the art of making excuses, is proficient at building on shaky foundations, never bullies anyone in public, excels at junking friends and works closely with his wife Moi Moi who is many years younger than him but not as photogenic. Two other best-selling books, "How to Survive Australia" and "How to be Normal in Australia" are turning him into a millionaire.

MARK KNIGHT

Mark Knight... political cartoonist, has commented on subjects from the Australian economy to the personalities of politicians in the national press. He owes his success to his mother who saw enough potential in his early scribblings to take them to a newspaper editor. Born in Marrickville, New South Wales, he is now the owner of fifteen devoted horses and is eminently qualified to pictorialize the ambitions of the Australian psyche.